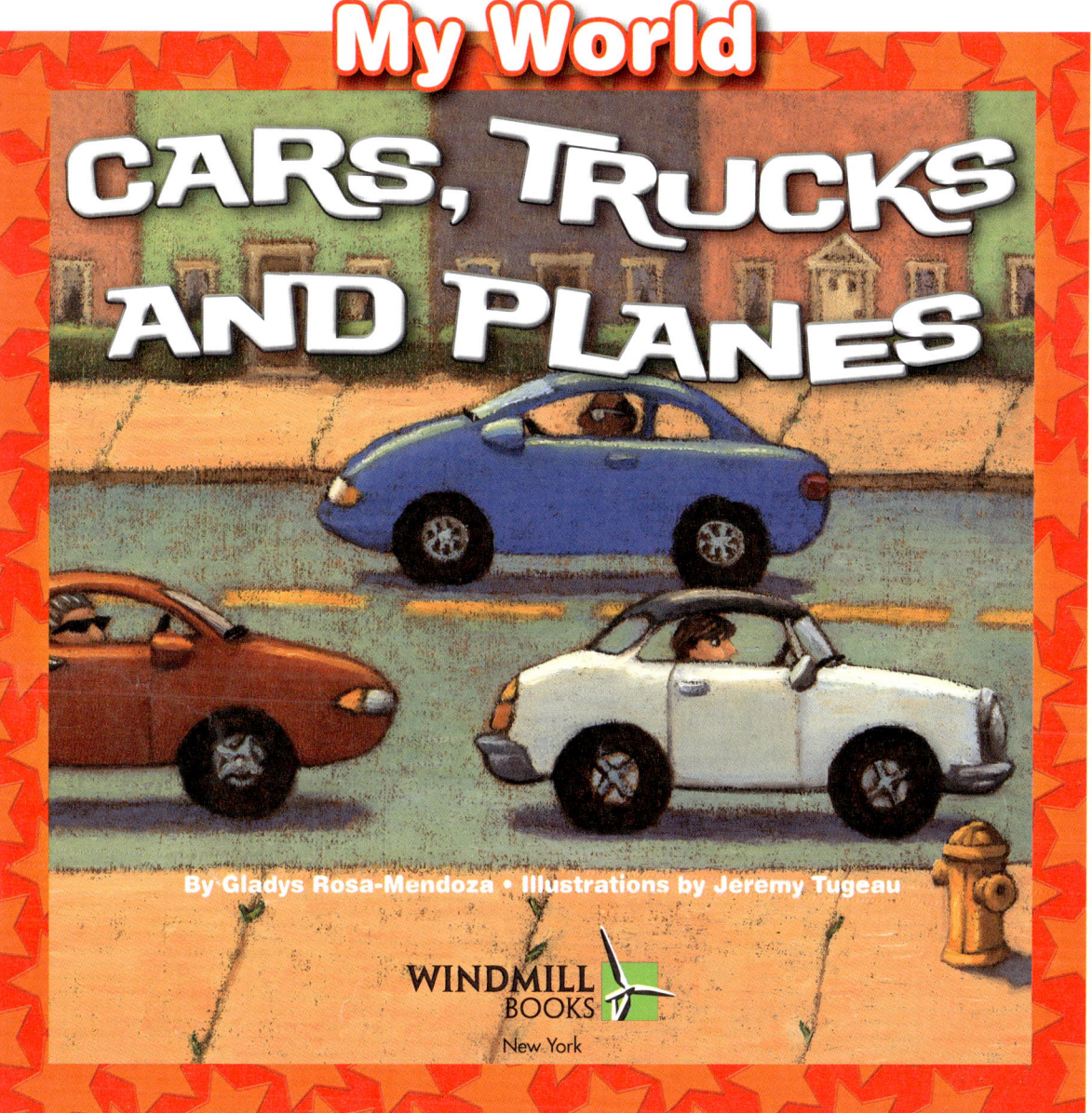

Published in 2011 by Windmill Books, LLC
303 Park Avenue South, Suite # 1280, New York, NY 10010-3657

Adaptations to North American Edition © 2011 Windmill Books, LLC
First published by me+mi publishing, inc. © 2004
Text and illustrations copyright © me+mi publishing, inc., 2004

All rights reserved. No part of this book may be reproduced in any form without permission in writing from the publisher, except by a reviewer.

CREDITS:
Author: Gladys Rosa-Mendoza
Illustrator: Jeremy Tugeau

Library of Congress Cataloging-in-Publication Data

Rosa-Mendoza, Gladys.
 Cars, trucks, and planes / by Gladys Rosa-Mendoza ; illustrated by Jeremy Tugeau. — School & library ed.
   p. cm. — (My world)
 Includes index.
 ISBN 978-1-60754-949-9 (library binding) — ISBN 978-1-61533-031-7 (pbk.) — ISBN 978-1-61533-032-4 (6-pack)
 1. Motor vehicles—Juvenile literature. I. Tugeau, Jeremy. II. Title.
 TL147.R647 2010
 629.04'6—dc22
                    2009054404

Manufactured in the United States of America

For more great fiction and nonfiction, go to www.windmillbooks.com

CPSIA Compliance Information: Batch #S10W: For further information contact Windmill Books, New York, New York at 1-866-478-0556.

Contents

On the Move	4
Read More!	20
Learn More!	21
Words to Know	22
Index	24
Web Sites	24

People get around many different ways. Here people are driving cars.

There is a red car, a white car, and a blue car.

The kids are getting to school on a yellow school bus.

The family is riding their bikes in the park.

Look at them rolling down the hill!

The man is driving a red truck.

The truck is carrying vegetables to the grocery store.

Planes fly high
in the sky.

They take people on long trips.

The train is taking people into the city.

They are going to work.

Look at the boats in the harbor.

The boats fly colorful flags.

Read More!

Nonfiction

Hubbell, Patricia. *Cars: Rushing! Honking! Zooming!*. Tarrytown, NY: Marshall Cavendish, 2006.

Mitton, Tony and Ant Parker. *Amazing Airplanes*. New York: Kingfisher, 2005.

Fiction

Calmenson, Stephanie. *Late For School!*. Minneapolis, MN: Carolrhoda Books, 2008.

Van Dusen, Chris. *If I Built a Car*. New York: Puffin, 2007.

Wilson, Adrienne C. *Isaac and the Bah Family Tree*. Mustang, OK: Tate Publishing, 2008.

Learn More!

 The first cars did not have a steering wheel!

 A bike that has three wheels is called a tricycle.

 A bike with a motor is called a motorcycle.

How does your family get around? How many different ways could you get to school?

Words to Know

bikes (byks) a vehicle with two wheels and pedals

city (SIH-tee) a place that is larger than a town, and usually has lots of buildings and people

boats (bohts) vehicles that travel on water

harbor (HAR-ber) an area of water where ships can dock

cars (kars) vehicles with four wheels and a motor

park (park) an area of land where people can play

plane (playn) a vehicle with wings that can travel through the sky

train (trayn) a vehicle that travels along a track

school (skoowl) the place where people go to learn new things

truck (truk) a large vehicle with wheels and a motor that can be used to move things

school bus (skoowl bus) a large vehicle that drives students to school

Index

B
bikes...8
boats...16

C
cars...4
city...14

H
harbor...16

P
park...8
plane...12

S
school...6
school bus...6

T
train...14
truck...10

Web Sites

For Web resources related to the subject of this book, go to:
www.windmillbooks.com/weblinks and select this book's title